The Curse
Is Not Greater Than
THE BLESSING

Rodney M. Howard-Browne, Th. D., D.Min., D.D.

Revival Ministries International

Tampa, Florida

Unless otherwise indicated, all scriptural references are from the King James Version of the Bible.

The Curse Is Not Greater Than the Blessing
ISBN: 978-1-62890-899-2

Copyright © 2004 by
Rodney M. Howard-Browne
P.O. Box 292888
Tampa, FL 33687 U.S.A.

Published by
Revival Ministries International
P.O. Box 292888
Tampa, FL 33687 U.S.A.

Printed in the United States of America.

All rights reserved under International Copyright Law. Contents and/or cover may not be reproduced in whole or in part in any form without the express written consent of the publisher.

Dedication

To the saints,

Remember, the curse is to the 3rd and 4th generation; however, the blessing is to a thousand (1000) generations.

Contents

Dedication iii

Introduction 1

Chapter One
The Myth 3

Chapter Two
The Curse 7

Chapter Three
The Blessing 27

Chapter Four
Choose – It's Up to You 33

Chapter Five
Some of My Favorite Psalms 45

Introduction

I felt led of the Lord to write this minibook because of the myths that are going around the body of Christ concerning curses. These myths run the gamut, involving everything from generational curses to curses placed on people by others. I regularly encounter people in the prayer lines who desire prayer for a generational curse or some kind of a curse to be broken off of them when this is not their problem at all. Many of them are totally paranoid about these "curses"–their lives manipulated by this misconception. Most of the time their biggest problem is their lack of knowledge of the Word of God–and their ignorance of the promises that are theirs!

The Lord dropped this phrase into my heart one day–"The curse is not greater than the blessing!"

I trust that as you prayerfully read this book the Lord will open your eyes so that you will be able to clearly see all that heaven has purchased for you at Calvary. I have included many scriptures in the book so that you can see that this is God's Word and not simply my opinion. The Scripture is plain—we must read it and believe it.

Chapter One

The Myth

One of the myths floating around the body of Christ is the Myth concerning curses. There are those that believe that curses are so powerful that they can destroy the life of the believer; however, one must remember that the devil uses fear to manipulate and control the life of anyone that will give place to it. How does a curse affect a believer? Should we be afraid of curses? What about generational curses?

The Believer – the Blessed of the Lord

When we are born again, we are translated out of the kingdom of darkness and translated into the kingdom of Light. The devil has no more authority over us other than the authority that we give him.

Colossians 1:13

13 Who hath delivered us from the power of darkness, and hath translated us into the kingdom of his dear Son.

We have been bought with a price and redeemed and no longer belong to the power of darkness, we belong to the kingdom of God. We are children of the living God. We are children of the light. There is not enough darkness to put out the smallest light. Some might argue well the devil this and the devil that, however the devil cannot touch us when we are walking in the light. The only time that he can touch us is when we open the door to him by not walking according to the Word of God.

The fact of the matter is that when God blessed you nothing can be done to reverse it.

Numbers 23:19-20

19 God is not a man, that he should lie; neither the son of man, that he should repent: hath he said, and shall he not do it? or hath he spoken, and shall he not make it good?

20 Behold, I have received commandment to bless: and he hath blessed; and I cannot reverse it.

In the new covenant this is confirmed by the fact that God hath blessed us with all spiritual blessings in Christ.

Ephesians 1:3

> 3 Blessed be the God and Father of our Lord Jesus Christ, who hath blessed us with all spiritual blessings in heavenly places in Christ.

In Christ we have these blessings and the curse cannot touch us. We have been blessed with all of heaven's blessings, this is not something that needs to happen, this is something that has already taken place. We need to walk as believers in the finished work of the cross.

When we as believers believe that the curse is powerful we underestimate the power of the cross, the power of the blood and the power of the resurrection thus making weak the finished work of the cross of Jesus Christ.

Colossians 2:15

15 And having spoiled principalities and powers, he made a shew of them openly, triumphing over them in it.

Jesus defeated the devil at Calvary and broke the power of the curse.

Chapter Two

The Curse

The Curse can be broken down into several areas:

- a. Generational Curses – those passed down from Generation to Generation.

- b. Curses in the Scripture – those promises of God that if you disobey Him and serve other gods and walk in rebellion then…

- c. Modern Day Curses – those curses that are cast as spells upon people by way of witchcraft, or a hateful person.

I will deal with these three in this chapter.

Firstly, curses cannot just come without a cause or a reason.

Proverbs 26:2

2 As the bird by wandering, as the swallow by flying, so the curse causeless shall not come.

The Living Bible says this:

Proverbs 26:2

> 2 An undeserved curse has no effect. Its intended victim will be no more harmed by it than by a sparrow or swallow flitting through the sky.

The undeserved curse has no effect–its intended victim will not be harmed–it will be as a bird flying over one's head–that takes care of the thought that curses are just flying around attaching themselves to people indiscriminately. The reasons why many believers are effected by curses I believe is:

1. Fear

2. The lack of knowledge of the Word of God

3. Not understanding the Father's love in relationship to the new covenant

No. 1 - Fear

Fear is a terrible thing, gripping at the minds and hearts of anyone who will open the door. It is so in Africa and other parts of the world where people practice witchcraft and fear is a common factor that gives the witch doctor the power over them. In Africa and Australia for example, if the witch doctor arrives in a village and sings and chants and throws bones then everyone knows in that village that someone is going to die. The next morning sure enough someone will have died. This is common. What killed those people? Simply this—Fear.

Job 3:25

> 25 For the thing which I greatly feared is come upon me, and that which I was afraid of is come unto me.

No. 2 - The Lack of Knowledge of God's Word

The reason that I say this is because if you are a child of God Almighty then you have to realize that the Devil has very limited power over you. The only power that he has over you is the power you give him.

Hosea 4:6

> 6 My people are destroyed for lack of knowledge: because thou hast rejected knowledge, I will also reject thee, that thou shalt be no priest to me: seeing thou hast forgotten the law of thy God, I will also forget thy children.

THE REASON THEY ARE DESTROYED IS BECAUSE OF THEIR LACK OF KNOWLEDGE of the Word of God.

2 Timothy 2:15

> 15 Study to shew thyself approved unto God, a workman that needeth not to be ashamed, rightly dividing the word of truth.

We must find out what God's Word says and then appropriate the promises in our lives. Remember this, the devil knows the scripture because he quoted it to Eve as well as Jesus. Hath God said, and if thou be the Son of God then....he misquoted the scripture. He loves to twist the scripture and to get you as the believer to think that God is not for you and that He is against you. As a new believer we must realize that we are new creations in Christ Jesus; old things have passed away, all things are new.

2 Corinthians 5:17

17 Therefore if any man be in Christ, he is a new creature: old things are passed away; behold, all things are become new.

This means that as a child of God the day that we are born again we are made new–a new creature–a new species that has never existed before–the old is passed away the new has come. We are a new generation–a chosen generation—a royal priesthood.

1 Peter 2:9

9 But ye are a chosen generation, a royal priesthood, an holy nation, a peculiar people; that ye should shew forth the praises of him who hath called you out of darkness into his marvellous light.

A peculiar people–with a special anointing. Notice that the scripture says that you should show forth the praises of Him who hath called you out of darkness into His marvelous light. This means there is a difference. Light versus darkness. You are different, changed.

An interesting account comes out of Africa, of a young lady who had been dedicated to witchcraft as a baby. Every night an owl would fly into the window and feed her some liquid. This liquid would paralyze her and the owl would transform into a demon who would then have intercourse with her. This went on for a number of years, the young lady unable to do anything about it. One day she was taken to a large open air crusade, that day she heard the gospel preached for the very first time. As the altar call was given she then responded and gave her life to Jesus and made Him Lord of her life. The following evening the owl returned and then spoke to her. This is what he said. "All these years you have been mine, however tonight I see that you are no longer mine, that you belong to Jesus, I see His blood over you. I will never be back," and with that he left and was never seen again.

Thank God for the power of the blood of Jesus Christ. Thank God for the New Birth, and thank God for the new creation.

No. 3 -
Not Understanding the Father's Love in Relationship to the New Covenant

2 Timothy 2:15

> 15 Study to shew thyself approved unto God, a workman that needeth not to be ashamed, rightly dividing the word of truth.

The reason why this verse is so important is because the scripture says to rightly divide the Word. How can that happen? We must study God's Word. Rightly divide–what does that mean? Well you will be amazed how many of God's children don't know the difference between the old and the new testament (covenant). What happens is that they take a little of the old and mix it with the new and come up with their own covenant. One minute they are under the Law, the next they are under grace and they become double-minded and have no clue–they remind me of a Canadian goose lost in a thunderstorm trying to find its way. They end up going from bondage back to freedom and then back to bondage. They don't understand the heart of the Father God and His great Love for His Children.

Jesus came to pay the price for our complete redemption.

Let's take some time and look at what Jesus redeemed us from and the curses that result from disobedience to God and His Word. These are in fact promises – promises to those who would disobey the Word of the Lord.

Deuteronomy 28:14-68

> 14 And thou shalt not go aside from any of the words which I command thee this day, to the right hand, or to the left, to go after other gods to serve them.
>
> 15 But it shall come to pass, if thou wilt not hearken unto the voice of the LORD thy God, to observe to do all his commandments and his statutes which I command thee this day; that all these curses shall come upon thee, and overtake thee:

If you will not listen to the Lord then these curses will be yours:

> 16 Cursed shalt thou be in the city, and cursed shalt thou be in the field.
>
> 17 Cursed shall be thy basket and thy store.
>
> 18 Cursed shall be the fruit of thy body, and the fruit of thy land, the increase of thy kine, and the flocks of thy sheep.

19 Cursed shalt thou be when thou comest in, and cursed shalt thou be when thou goest out.

20 The LORD shall send upon thee cursing, vexation, and rebuke, in all that thou settest thine hand unto for to do, until thou be destroyed, and until thou perish quickly; because of the wickedness of thy doings, whereby thou hast forsaken me.

21 The LORD shall make the pestilence cleave unto thee, until he have consumed thee from off the land, whither thou goest to possess it.

22 The LORD shall smite thee with a consumption, and with a fever, and with an inflammation, and with an extreme burning, and with the sword, and with blasting, and with mildew; and they shall pursue thee until thou perish.

23 And thy heaven that is over thy head shall be brass, and the earth that is under thee shall be iron. 24 The LORD shall make the rain of thy land powder and dust: from heaven shall it come down upon thee, until thou be destroyed.

25 The LORD shall cause thee to be smitten before thine enemies: thou shalt go out one way against them, and flee seven ways before them: and shalt be removed into all the kingdoms of the earth.

26 And thy carcase shall be meat unto all fowls of the air, and unto the beasts of the earth, and no man shall fray them away.

27 The LORD will smite thee with the botch of Egypt, and with the emerods, and with the scab, and with the itch, whereof thou canst not be healed.

28 The LORD shall smite thee with madness, and blindness, and astonishment of heart:

29 And thou shalt grope at noonday, as the blind gropeth in darkness, and thou shalt not prosper in thy ways: and thou shalt be only oppressed and spoiled evermore, and no man shall save thee.

30 Thou shalt betroth a wife, and another man shall lie with her: thou shalt build an house, and thou shalt not dwell therein: thou shalt plant a vineyard, and shalt not gather the grapes thereof.

31 Thine ox shall be slain before thine eyes, and thou shalt not eat thereof: thine ass shall be violently taken away from before thy face, and shall not be restored to thee: thy sheep shall be given unto thine enemies, and thou shalt have none to rescue them.

32 Thy sons and thy daughters shall be given unto another people, and thine eyes shall look, and fail with longing for them all the day long: and there shall be no might in thine hand.

33 The fruit of thy land, and all thy labours, shall a nation which thou knowest not eat up; and thou shalt be only oppressed and crushed alway:

34 So that thou shalt be mad for the sight of thine eyes which thou shalt see.

35 The LORD shall smite thee in the knees, and in the legs, with a sore botch that cannot be healed, from the sole of thy foot unto the top of thy head.

36 The LORD shall bring thee, and thy king which thou shalt set over thee, unto a nation which neither thou nor thy fathers have

known; and there shalt thou serve other gods, wood and stone.

37 And thou shalt become an astonishment, a proverb, and a byword, among all nations whither the LORD shall lead thee.

38 Thou shalt carry much seed out into the field, and shalt gather but little in; for the locust shall consume it.

39 Thou shalt plant vineyards, and dress them, but shalt neither drink of the wine, nor gather the grapes; for the worms shall eat them.

40 Thou shalt have olive trees throughout all thy coasts, but thou shalt not anoint thyself with the oil; for thine olive shall cast his fruit.

41 Thou shalt beget sons and daughters, but thou shalt not enjoy them; for they shall go into captivity. 42 All thy trees and fruit of thy land shall the locust consume.

43 The stranger that is within thee shall get up above thee very high; and thou shalt come down very low.

44 He shall lend to thee, and thou shalt not lend to him: he shall be the head, and thou shalt be the tail.

45 Moreover all these curses shall come upon thee, and shall pursue thee, and overtake thee, till thou be destroyed; because thou hearkenedst not unto the voice of the LORD thy God, to keep his commandments and his statutes which he commanded thee:

46 And they shall be upon thee for a sign and for a wonder, and upon thy seed for ever. 47 Because thou servedst not the LORD thy God with joyfulness, and with gladness of heart, for the abundance of all things;

Because you do not serve the Lord with Joyfulness and with gladness of heart………you are in trouble.

48 Therefore shalt thou serve thine enemies which the LORD shall send against thee, in hunger, and in thirst, and in nakedness, and in want of all things: and he shall put a yoke of iron upon thy neck, until he have destroyed thee.

The Yoke upon your neck–this yoke is the same yoke that Jesus came to destroy. This yoke is the same yoke that the anointing will destroy.

> 49 The LORD shall bring a nation against thee from far, from the end of the earth, as swift as the eagle flieth; a nation whose tongue thou shalt not understand;
>
> 50 A nation of fierce countenance, which shall not regard the person of the old, nor shew favour to the young:
>
> 51 And he shall eat the fruit of thy cattle, and the fruit of thy land, until thou be destroyed: which also shall not leave thee either corn, wine, or oil, or the increase of thy kine, or flocks of thy sheep, until he have destroyed thee.
>
> 52 And he shall besiege thee in all thy gates, until thy high and fenced walls come down, wherein thou trustedst, throughout all thy land: and he shall besiege thee in all thy gates throughout all thy land, which the LORD thy God hath given thee.
>
> 53 And thou shalt eat the fruit of thine own body, the flesh of thy sons and of thy daughters, which the LORD thy God hath

given thee, in the siege, and in the straitness, wherewith thine enemies shall distress thee:

54 So that the man that is tender among you, and very delicate, his eye shall be evil toward his brother, and toward the wife of his bosom, and toward the remnant of his children which he shall leave:

55 So that he will not give to any of them of the flesh of his children whom he shall eat: because he hath nothing left him in the siege, and in the straitness, wherewith thine enemies shall distress thee in all thy gates.

56 The tender and delicate woman among you, which would not adventure to set the sole of her foot upon the ground for delicateness and tenderness, her eye shall be evil toward the husband of her bosom, and toward her son, and toward her daughter,

57 And toward her young one that cometh out from between her feet, and toward her children which she shall bear: for she shall eat them for want of all things secretly in the siege and straitness, wherewith thine enemy shall distress thee in thy gates.

58 If thou wilt not observe to do all the words of this law that are written in this book, that thou mayest fear this glorious and fearful name, THE LORD THY GOD;

59 Then the LORD will make thy plagues wonderful, and the plagues of thy seed, even great plagues, and of long continuance, and sore sicknesses, and of long continuance.

60 Moreover he will bring upon thee all the diseases of Egypt, which thou wast afraid of; and they shall cleave unto thee.

61 Also every sickness, and every plague, which is not written in the book of this law, them will the LORD bring upon thee, until thou be destroyed.

62 And ye shall be left few in number, whereas ye were as the stars of heaven for multitude; because thou wouldest not obey the voice of the LORD thy God.

63 And it shall come to pass, that as the LORD rejoiced over you to do you good, and to multiply you; so the LORD will rejoice over you to destroy you, and to bring you to nought; and ye shall be plucked from off the land whither thou goest to possess it.

64 And the LORD shall scatter thee among all people, from the one end of the earth even unto the other; and there thou shalt serve other gods, which neither thou nor thy fathers have known, even wood and stone.

65 And among these nations shalt thou find no ease, neither shall the sole of thy foot have rest: but the LORD shall give thee there a trembling heart, and failing of eyes, and sorrow of mind:

66 And thy life shall hang in doubt before thee; and thou shalt fear day and night, and shalt have none assurance of thy life:

67 In the morning thou shalt say, Would God it were even! and at even thou shalt say, Would God it were morning! for the fear of thine heart wherewith thou shalt fear, and for the sight of thine eyes which thou shalt see.

68 And the LORD shall bring thee into Egypt again with ships, by the way whereof I spake unto thee, Thou shalt see it no more again: and there ye shall be sold unto your enemies for bondmen and bondwomen, and no man shall buy you.

It is evident that from this passage we can see every curse imaginable and somehow because of religion and tradition, we think that this is our lot, not realizing that Jesus on Calvary purchased our freedom, so that we could live and not die. It does not even make common sense to believe Jesus would save us from eternal damnation and Hell and then make us live in Hell all the way until we get to heaven. I don't believe this for one moment.

There are those who would read this passage of Deuteronomy 28 and not realize that God specifically says that if you listen to Him and obey His Word then these curses will have no place in your life. He says all these blessings (we'll discuss the blessings in the next chapter). The curse is not greater than the blessing.

Exodus 20:5

> 5 Thou shalt not bow down thyself to them, nor serve them: for I the LORD thy God am a jealous God, visiting the iniquity of the fathers upon the children unto the third and fourth generation of them that hate me.

The curse God says is unto the third and fourth generation of them that hate Me. This is very evident that the curse is to those that hate the Lord not to His children. He Loves us so much and wants to bless us more than we want to be blessed. He has made every provision for our blessing. This was made manifest at the cross of Calvary.

As children of the living God we have absolutely nothing to fear from the curse because Jesus has come to bring us into the Blessing.

Chapter Three

The Blessing

The Blessing can be broken down into several areas:

a. Generational Blessings – those passed down from Generation to Generation – to 1000 generations of those that fear God.

b. Blessings in the Scripture – those promises of God that if you obey Him and serve Him then all these blessings will be yours.

c. Modern Day Blessings – those blessings that are pronounced upon people by anointed men of God speaking by way of the anointing or a father blessing his children, etc.

I will discuss all three in this chapter.

In order to receive the blessing we need to know that Jesus has redeemed us from the curse of the Law. The curse of the Law was threefold.

Galatians 3:13-14

13 Christ hath redeemed us from the curse of the law, being made a curse for us: for it is written, Cursed is every one that hangeth on a tree:

14 That the blessing of Abraham might come on the Gentiles through Jesus Christ; that we might receive the promise of the Spirit through faith.

Deuteronomy 28:1-13

1 And it shall come to pass, if thou shalt hearken diligently unto the voice of the LORD thy God, to observe and to do all his commandments which I command thee this day, that the LORD thy God will set thee on high above all nations of the earth.

This is the exact opposite of the curse–if you listen to the Lord and obey Him then these blessings shall be yours.

2 And all these blessings shall come on thee, and overtake thee, if thou shalt hearken unto the voice of the LORD thy God.

3 Blessed shalt thou be in the city, and blessed shalt thou be in the field.

4 Blessed shall be the fruit of thy body, and the fruit of thy ground, and the fruit of thy cattle, the increase of thy kine, and the flocks of thy sheep.

5 Blessed shall be thy basket and thy store.

6 Blessed shalt thou be when thou comest in, and blessed shalt thou be when thou goest out.

7 The LORD shall cause thine enemies that rise up against thee to be smitten before thy face: they shall come out against thee one way, and flee before thee seven ways.

8 The LORD shall command the blessing upon thee in thy storehouses, and in all that thou settest thine hand unto; and he shall bless thee in the land which the LORD thy God giveth thee.

9 The LORD shall establish thee an holy people unto himself, as he hath sworn unto thee, if thou shalt keep the commandments of the LORD thy God, and walk in his ways.

10 And all people of the earth shall see that thou art called by the name of the LORD; and they shall be afraid of thee.

11 And the LORD shall make thee plenteous in goods, in the fruit of thy body, and in the fruit of thy cattle, and in the fruit of thy ground, in the land which the LORD sware unto thy fathers to give thee.

12 The LORD shall open unto thee his good treasure, the heaven to give the rain unto thy land in his season, and to bless all the work of thine hand: and thou shalt lend unto many nations, and thou shalt not borrow.

13 And the LORD shall make thee the head, and not the tail; and thou shalt be above only, and thou shalt not be beneath; if that thou hearken unto the commandments of the LORD thy God, which I command thee this day, to observe and to do them.

If we are obedient to obey God and walk in His ways then these blessings are ours–the Word of God declares that in:

Psalm 105:8

8 He hath remembered his covenant for ever, the word which he commanded to a thousand generations.

His blessings are to a thousand generations.

Deuteronomy 7:9

> 9 Know therefore that the LORD thy God, he is God, the faithful God, which keepeth covenant and mercy with them that love him and keep his commandments to a thousand generations.

A thousand generations of them that Love the Lord.

Exodus 20:5-6

> 5 Thou shalt not bow down thyself to them, nor serve them: for I the LORD thy God am a jealous God, visiting the iniquity of the fathers upon the children unto the third and fourth generation of them that hate me;
>
> 6 And shewing mercy unto thousands of them that love me, and keep my commandments.

The curse is to the third and fourth generations of them that hate God but the Blessing is unto a thousand generations of them that Love Him and keep His commandments.

The Curse is not greater than the Blessing!

Chapter Four

Choose – It's Up to You

God spoke to the children of Israel plainly and He gave them a choice–He basically said to them–you choose.

Deuteronomy 30:19

> 19 I call heaven and earth to record this day against you, that I have set before you life and death, blessing and cursing: therefore choose life, that both thou and thy seed may live.

The Lord has plans for His people, plans to bless them, not plans to harm them at all as long as they obey Him and remember Him and walk in His Word and keep His commandments and not forget Him.

Deuteronomy 8:1-9:1

> 8:1 All the commandments which I command thee this day shall ye observe to do, that ye may live, and multiply, and go in and possess

the land which the LORD sware unto your fathers.

2 And thou shalt remember all the way which the LORD thy God led thee these forty years in the wilderness, to humble thee, and to prove thee, to know what was in thine heart, whether thou wouldest keep his commandments, or no.

3 And he humbled thee, and suffered thee to hunger, and fed thee with manna, which thou knewest not, neither did thy fathers know; that he might make thee know that man doth not live by bread only, but by every word that proceedeth out of the mouth of the LORD doth man live.

4 Thy raiment waxed not old upon thee, neither did thy foot swell, these forty years.

5 Thou shalt also consider in thine heart, that, as a man chasteneth his son, so the LORD thy God chasteneth thee.

6 Therefore thou shalt keep the commandments of the LORD thy God, to walk in his ways, and to fear him.

Notice in the following verses how the Lord is bringing you into a blessed and prosperous place.

7 For the LORD thy God bringeth thee into a good land, a land of brooks of water, of fountains and depths that spring out of valleys and hills;

8 A land of wheat, and barley, and vines, and fig trees, and pomegranates; a land of oil olive, and honey;

9 A land wherein thou shalt eat bread without scarceness, thou shalt not lack any thing in it; a land whose stones are iron, and out of whose hills thou mayest dig brass. You will not lack anything!

10 When thou hast eaten and art full, then thou shalt bless the LORD thy God for the good land which he hath given thee.

The dangers of forgetting God and losing sight of the fact that He has blessed you!

11 Beware that thou forget not the LORD thy God, in not keeping his commandments, and his judgments, and his statutes, which I command thee this day:

12 Lest when thou hast eaten and art full, and hast built goodly houses, and dwelt therein;

> 13 And when thy herds and thy flocks multiply, and thy silver and thy gold is multiplied, and all that thou hast is multiplied;
>
> 14 Then thine heart be lifted up, and thou forget the LORD thy God, which brought thee forth out of the land of Egypt, from the house of bondage.

This is so easy when you have:

1. Eaten and are full.
2. Built great houses and lived in them.
3. Your herds and flocks multiply.
4. Silver and gold is multiplied.
5. All that you have is multiplied.

Then you get arrogant and proud and forget God.

> 15 Who led thee through that great and terrible wilderness, wherein were fiery serpents, and scorpions, and drought, where there was no water; who brought thee forth water out of the rock of flint;
>
> 16 Who fed thee in the wilderness with manna, which thy fathers knew not, that he

might humble thee, and that he might prove thee, to do thee good at thy latter end.

Don't forget God!

17 And thou say in thine heart, My power and the might of mine hand hath gotten me this wealth.

18 But thou shalt remember the LORD thy God: for it is he that giveth thee power to get wealth, that he may establish his covenant which he sware unto thy fathers, as it is this day.

It is the Lord your God that gives you the anointing, ability to create wealth, in order that He might establish His covenant.

19 And it shall be, if thou do at all forget the LORD thy God, and walk after other gods, and serve them, and worship them, I testify against you this day that ye shall surely perish.

20 As the nations which the LORD destroyeth before your face, so shall ye perish; because ye would not be obedient unto the voice of the LORD your God.

The 30th chapter of the book of Deuteronomy is a powerful chapter because it is clearly God's plan to bless His children.

Deuteronomy 30:1-31:1

> 30:1 And it shall come to pass, when all these things are come upon thee, the blessing and the curse, which I have set before thee, and thou shalt call them to mind among all the nations, whither the LORD thy God hath driven thee,
>
> 2 And shalt return unto the LORD thy God, and shalt obey his voice according to all that I command thee this day, thou and thy children, with all thine heart, and with all thy soul;
>
> 3 That then the LORD thy God will turn thy captivity, and have compassion upon thee, and will return and gather thee from all the nations, whither the LORD thy God hath scattered thee.
>
> 4 If any of thine be driven out unto the outmost parts of heaven, from thence will the LORD thy God gather thee, and from thence will he fetch thee:
>
> 5 And the LORD thy God will bring thee into the land which thy fathers possessed, and thou

shalt possess it; and he will do thee good, and multiply thee above thy fathers.

6 And the LORD thy God will circumcise thine heart, and the heart of thy seed, to love the LORD thy God with all thine heart, and with all thy soul, that thou mayest live.

7 And the LORD thy God will put all these curses upon thine enemies, and on them that hate thee, which persecuted thee.

The curses are for your enemies–not you.

8 And thou shalt return and obey the voice of the LORD, and do all his commandments which I command thee this day.

9 And the LORD thy God will make thee plenteous in every work of thine hand, in the fruit of thy body, and in the fruit of thy cattle, and in the fruit of thy land, for good: for the LORD will again rejoice over thee for good, as he rejoiced over thy fathers:

This sounds like extreme blessing–what do you say?

10 If thou shalt hearken unto the voice of the LORD thy God, to keep his commandments and his statutes which are written in this book

> of the law, and if thou turn unto the LORD thy God with all thine heart, and with all thy soul.
>
> 11 For this commandment which I command thee this day, it is not hidden from thee, neither is it far off.

God says that this commandment is not something far away–it is right in front of you.

> 12 It is not in heaven, that thou shouldest say, Who shall go up for us to heaven, and bring it unto us, that we may hear it, and do it?
>
> 13 Neither is it beyond the sea, that thou shouldest say, Who shall go over the sea for us, and bring it unto us, that we may hear it, and do it?
>
> 14 But the word is very nigh unto thee, in thy mouth, and in thy heart, that thou mayest do it.

The Word is nigh you in your mouth and in your heart, so that you can do it.

> 15 See, I have set before thee this day life and good, and death and evil;

Life and Good or Death and Evil–what will it be? The choice is yours.

16 In that I command thee this day to love the LORD thy God, to walk in his ways, and to keep his commandments and his statutes and his judgments, that thou mayest live and multiply: and the LORD thy God shall bless thee in the land whither thou goest to possess it.

17 But if thine heart turn away, so that thou wilt not hear, but shalt be drawn away, and worship other gods, and serve them;

If you listen and obey, you will be blessed–if you don't listen and obey, then you will die.

18 I denounce unto you this day, that ye shall surely perish, and that ye shall not prolong your days upon the land, whither thou passest over Jordan to go to possess it.

19 I call heaven and earth to record this day against you, that I have set before you life and death, blessing and cursing: therefore choose life, that both thou and thy seed may live:

The Choice is ours–what will it be?

Blessing or Cursing, it's up to you.

> 20 That thou mayest love the LORD thy God, and that thou mayest obey his voice, and that thou mayest cleave unto him: for he is thy life, and the length of thy days: that thou mayest dwell in the land which the LORD sware unto thy fathers, to Abraham, to Isaac, and to Jacob, to give them.

Things that you need to do to walk in God's Blessings Daily:

1. Realize that God is for you and not against you.

2. Walk in His Word and obey Him completely.

3. The Choice is yours, Blessing or cursing– it's up to you.

4. The curse will be far from you, because Christ hath redeemed you from the curse of the law. He has paid it in full.

5. The Blessings are to a thousand generations of them that fear God.

6. The curse is to the third and fourth generation of them that hate God.

7. The Curse is not greater than the Blessing.

Chapter Five

Some of My Favorite Psalms

Prerequisites for Blessing

Psalm 1

1 Blessed is the man that walketh not in the counsel of the ungodly, nor standeth in the way of sinners, nor sitteth in the seat of the scornful.

2 But his delight is in the law of the LORD; and in his law doth he meditate day and night.

3 And he shall be like a tree planted by the rivers of water, that bringeth forth his fruit in his season; his leaf also shall not wither; and whatsoever he doeth shall prosper.

My Deliverer

Psalm 3

1 LORD, how are they increased that trouble me! many are they that rise up against me.

2 Many there be which say of my soul, There is no help for him in God. Selah.

3 But thou, O LORD, art a shield for me; my glory, and the lifter up of mine head.

4 I cried unto the LORD with my voice, and he heard me out of his holy hill. Selah.

5 I laid me down and slept; I awaked; for the LORD sustained me.

6 I will not be afraid of ten thousands of people, that have set themselves against me round about.

7 Arise, O LORD; save me, O my God: for thou hast smitten all mine enemies upon the cheek bone; thou hast broken the teeth of the ungodly.

8 Salvation belongeth unto the LORD: thy blessing is upon thy people. Selah.

My Preservation

Psalm 16

1 Preserve me, O God: for in thee do I put my trust.

2 O my soul, thou hast said unto the LORD, Thou art my Lord: my goodness extendeth not to thee;

3 But to the saints that are in the earth, and to the excellent, in whom is all my delight.

4 Their sorrows shall be multiplied that hasten after another god: their drink offerings of blood will I not offer, nor take up their names into my lips.

5 The LORD is the portion of mine inheritance and of my cup: thou maintainest my lot.

6 The lines are fallen unto me in pleasant places; yea, I have a goodly heritage.

7 I will bless the LORD, who hath given me counsel: my reins also instruct me in the night seasons.

8 I have set the LORD always before me: because he is at my right hand, I shall not be moved.

9 Therefore my heart is glad, and my glory rejoiceth: my flesh also shall rest in hope.

10 For thou wilt not leave my soul in hell; neither wilt thou suffer thine Holy One to see corruption.

11 Thou wilt shew me the path of life: in thy presence is fulness of joy; at thy right hand there are pleasures for evermore.

My Shepherd–A Now Psalm –It's for Today

Psalm 23

1 The LORD is my shepherd; I shall not want.

2 He maketh me to lie down in green pastures: he leadeth me beside the still waters.

3 He restoreth my soul: he leadeth me in the paths of righteousness for his name's sake.

4 Yea, though I walk through the valley of the shadow of death, I will fear no evil: for thou art with me; thy rod and thy staff they comfort me.

5 Thou preparest a table before me in the presence of mine enemies: thou anointest my head with oil; my cup runneth over.

6 Surely goodness and mercy shall follow me all the days of my life: and I will dwell in the house of the LORD for ever.

Clean Hands and a Pure Heart
Psalm 24

1 The earth is the LORD's, and the fullness thereof; the world, and they that dwell therein.

2 For he hath founded it upon the seas, and established it upon the floods.

3 Who shall ascend into the hill of the LORD? or who shall stand in his holy place?

4 He that hath clean hands, and a pure heart; who hath not lifted up his soul unto vanity, nor sworn deceitfully.

5 He shall receive the blessing from the LORD, and righteousness from the God of his salvation.

6 This is the generation of them that seek him, that seek thy face, O Jacob. Selah.

7 Lift up your head, O ye gates; and be ye lift up, ye everlasting doors; and the King of glory shall come in.

8 Who is this King of glory? The LORD strong and mighty, the LORD mighty in battle.

9 Lift up your heads, O ye gates; even lift them up, ye everlasting doors; and the King of glory shall come in.

10 Who is this King of glory? The LORD of hosts, he is the King of glory. Selah.

Afraid of Nothing or No One –He's My Rock, My Shelter

Psalm 27

1 The LORD is my light and my salvation; whom shall I fear? the LORD is the strength of my life; of whom shall I be afraid?

2 When the wicked, even mine enemies and my foes, came upon me to eat up my flesh, they stumbled and fell.

3 Though an host should encamp against me, my heart shall not fear: though war should rise against me, in this will I be confident.

4 One thing have I desired of the LORD, that will I seek after; that I may dwell in the house of the LORD all the days of my life, to behold the beauty of the LORD, and to inquire in his temple.

5 For in the time of trouble he shall hide me in his pavilion: in the secret of his tabernacle shall he hide me; he shall set me up upon a rock.

6 And now shall mine head be lifted up above mine enemies round about me: therefore will I offer in his tabernacle sacrifices of joy; I will sing, yea, I will sing praises unto the LORD.

7 Hear, O LORD, when I cry with my voice: have mercy also upon me, and answer me.

8 When thou saidst, Seek ye my face; my heart said unto thee, Thy face, LORD, will I seek.

9 Hide not thy face far from me; put not thy servant away in anger: thou hast been my help; leave me not, neither forsake me, O God of my salvation.

10 When my father and my mother forsake me, then the LORD will take me up.

11 Teach me thy way, O LORD, and lead me in a plain path, because of mine enemies.

12 Deliver me not over unto the will of mine enemies: for false witnesses are risen up against me, and such as breathe out cruelty.

13 I had fainted, unless I had believed to see the goodness of the LORD in the land of the living.

14 Wait on the LORD: be of good courage, and he shall strengthen thine heart: wait, I say, on the LORD.

The Angels Are Around Me
Psalm 34

1 I will bless the LORD at all times: his praise shall continually be in my mouth.

2 My soul shall make her boast in the LORD: the humble shall hear thereof, and be glad.

3 O magnify the LORD with me, and let us exalt his name together.

4 I sought the LORD, and he heard me, and delivered me from all my fears.

5 They looked unto him, and were lightened: and their faces were not ashamed.

6 This poor man cried, and the LORD heard him, and saved him out of all his troubles.

7 The angel of the LORD encampeth round about them that fear him, and delivereth them.

8 O taste and see that the LORD is good: blessed is the man that trusteth in him.

9 O fear the LORD, ye his saints: for there is no want to them that fear him.

10 The young lions do lack, and suffer hunger: but they that seek the LORD shall not want any good thing.

11 Come, ye children, hearken unto me: I will teach you the fear of the LORD.

12 What man is he that desireth life, and loveth many days, that he may see good?

13 Keep thy tongue from evil, and thy lips from speaking guile.

14 Depart from evil, and do good; seek peace, and pursue it.

15 The eyes of the LORD are upon the righteous, and his ears are open unto their cry.

16 The face of the LORD is against them that do evil, to cut off the remembrance of them from the earth.

17 The righteous cry, and the LORD heareth, and delivereth them out of all their troubles.

18 The LORD is nigh unto them that are of a broken heart; and saveth such as be of a contrite spirit.

19 Many are the afflictions of the righteous: but the LORD delivereth him out of them all.

20 He keepeth all his bones: not one of them is broken.

21 Evil shall slay the wicked: and they that hate the righteous shall be desolate.

22 The LORD redeemeth the soul of his servants: and none of them that trust in him shall be desolate.

My Desire–My Lord and My God
Psalm 37

1 Fret not thyself because of evildoers, neither be thou envious against the workers of iniquity.

2 For they shall soon be cut down like the grass, and wither as the green herb.

3 Trust in the LORD, and do good; so shalt thou dwell in the land, and verily thou shalt be fed.

4 Delight thyself also in the LORD; and he shall give thee the desires of thine heart.

5 Commit thy way unto the LORD; trust also in him; and he shall bring it to pass.

6 And he shall bring forth thy righteousness as the light, and thy judgment as the noonday.

7 Rest in the LORD, and wait patiently for him: fret not thyself because of him who prospereth in his way, because of the man who bringeth wicked devices to pass.

8 Cease from anger, and forsake wrath: fret not thyself in any wise to do evil.

9 For evildoers shall be cut off: but those that wait upon the LORD, they shall inherit the earth.

10 For yet a little while, and the wicked shall not be: yea, thou shalt diligently consider his place, and it shall not be.

11 But the meek shall inherit the earth; and shall delight themselves in the abundance of peace.

12 The wicked plotteth against the just, and gnasheth upon him with his teeth.

13 The Lord shall laugh at him: for he seeth that his day is coming.

14 The wicked have drawn out the sword, and have bent their bow, to cast down the poor and needy, and to slay such as be of upright conversation.

15 Their sword shall enter into their own heart, and their bows shall be broken.

16 A little that a righteous man hath is better than the riches of many wicked.

17 For the arms of the wicked shall be broken: but the LORD upholdeth the righteous.

18 The LORD knoweth the days of the upright: and their inheritance shall be for ever.

19 They shall not be ashamed in the evil time: and in the days of famine they shall be satisfied.

20 But the wicked shall perish, and the enemies of the LORD shall be as the fat of lambs: they shall consume; into smoke shall they consume away.

21 The wicked borroweth, and payeth not again: but the righteous sheweth mercy, and giveth.

22 For such as be blessed of him shall inherit the earth; and they that be cursed of him shall be cut off.

23 The steps of a good man are ordered by the LORD: and he delighteth in his way.

24 Though he fall, he shall not be utterly cast down: for the LORD upholdeth him with his hand.

25 I have been young, and now am old; yet have I not seen the righteous forsaken, nor his seed begging bread.

26 He is ever merciful, and lendeth; and his seed is blessed.

27 Depart from evil, and do good; and dwell for evermore.

28 For the LORD loveth judgment, and forsaketh not his saints; they are preserved for ever: but the seed of the wicked shall be cut off.

29 The righteous shall inherit the land, and dwell therein for ever.

30 The mouth of the righteous speaketh wisdom, and his tongue talketh of judgment.

31 The law of his God is in his heart; none of his steps shall slide.

32 The wicked watcheth the righteous, and seeketh to slay him.

33 The LORD will not leave him in his hand, nor condemn him when he is judged.

34 Wait on the LORD, and keep his way, and he shall exalt thee to inherit the land: when the wicked are cut off, thou shalt see it.

35 I have seen the wicked in great power, and spreading himself like a green bay tree.

36 Yet he passed away, and, lo, he was not: yea, I sought him, but he could not be found.

37 Mark the perfect man, and behold the upright: for the end of that man is peace.

38 But the transgressors shall be destroyed together: the end of the wicked shall be cut off.

39 But the salvation of the righteous is of the LORD: he is their strength in the time of trouble.

40 And the LORD shall help them and deliver them: he shall deliver them from the wicked, and save them, because they trust in him.

I Am Kept Alive by the Lord, Because I Give to the Poor

Psalm 41

1 Blessed is he that considereth the poor: the LORD will deliver him in time of trouble.

2 The LORD will preserve him, and keep him alive; and he shall be blessed upon the earth: and thou wilt not deliver him unto the will of his enemies.

3 The LORD will strengthen him upon the bed of languishing: thou wilt make all his bed in his sickness.

4 I said, LORD, be merciful unto me: heal my soul; for I have sinned against thee.

5 Mine enemies speak evil of me, When shall he die, and his name perish?

6 And if he come to see me, he speaketh vanity: his heart gathereth iniquity to itself; when he goeth abroad, he telleth it.

7 All that hate me whisper together against me: against me do they devise my hurt.

8 An evil disease, say they, cleaveth fast unto him: and now that he lieth he shall rise up no more.

9 Yea, mine own familiar friend, in whom I trusted, which did eat of my bread, hath lifted up his heel against me.

10 But thou, O LORD, be merciful unto me, and raise me up, that I may requite them.

11 By this I know that thou favourest me, because mine enemy doth not triumph over me.

12 And as for me, thou upholdest me in mine integrity, and settest me before thy face for ever.

13 Blessed be the LORD God of Israel from everlasting, and to everlasting. Amen, and Amen.

Psalm 46

1 God is our refuge and strength, a very present in trouble.

2 Therefore will not we fear, though the earth be removed, and though the mountains be carried into the midst of the sea;

3 Though the waters thereof roar and be troubled, though the mountains shake with the swelling thereof. Selah.

4 There is a river, the streams whereof shall make glad the city of God, the holy place of the tabernacles of the most High.

5 God is in the midst of her; she shall not be moved: God shall help her, and that right early.

6 The heathen raged, the kingdoms were moved: he uttered his voice, the earth melted.

7 The LORD of hosts is with us; the God of Jacob is our refuge. Selah.

8 Come, behold the works of the LORD, what desolations he hath made in the earth.

9 He maketh wars to cease unto the end of the earth; he breaketh the bow, and cutteth the spear in sunder; he burneth the chariot in the fire.

10 Be still, and know that I am God: I will be exalted among the heathen, I will be exalted in the earth.

11 The LORD of hosts is with us; the God of Jacob is our refuge. Selah.

Living in the Secret Place
Psalm 91

1 He that dwelleth in the secret place of the most High shall abide under the shadow of the Almighty.

2 I will say of the LORD, He is my refuge and my fortress: my God; in him will I trust.

3 Surely he shall deliver thee from the snare of the fowler, and from the noisome pestilence.

4 He shall cover thee with his feathers, and under his wings shalt thou trust: his truth shall be thy shield and buckler.

5 Thou shalt not be afraid for the terror by night; nor for the arrow that flieth by day;

6 Nor for the pestilence that walketh in darkness; nor for the destruction that wasteth at noonday.

7 A thousand shall fall at thy side, and ten thousand at thy right hand; but it shall not come nigh thee.

8 Only with thine eyes shalt thou behold and see the reward of the wicked.

9 Because thou hast made the LORD, which is my refuge, even the most High, thy habitation;

10 There shall no evil befall thee, neither shall any plague come nigh thy dwelling.

11 For he shall give his angels charge over thee, to keep thee in all thy ways.

12 They shall bear thee up in their hands, lest thou dash thy foot against a stone.

13 Thou shalt tread upon the lion and adder: the young lion and the dragon shalt thou trample under feet.

14 Because he hath set his love upon me, therefore will I deliver him: I will set him on high, because he hath known my name.

15 He shall call upon me, and I will answer him: I will be with him in trouble; I will deliver him, and honour him.

16 With long life will I satisfy him, and shew him my salvation.

Psalm 92

1 It is a good thing to give thanks unto the LORD, and to sing praises unto thy name, O most High:

2 To shew forth thy lovingkindness in the morning, and thy faithfulness every night,

3 Upon an instrument of ten strings, and upon the psaltery; upon the harp with a solemn sound.

4 For thou, LORD, hast made me glad through thy work: I will triumph in the works of thy hands.

5 O LORD, how great are thy works! and thy thoughts are very deep.

6 A brutish man knoweth not; neither doth a fool understand this.

7 When the wicked spring as the grass, and when all the workers of iniquity do flourish; it is that they shall be destroyed for ever:

8 But thou, LORD, art most high for evermore.

9 For, lo, thine enemies, O LORD, for, lo, thine enemies shall perish; all the workers of iniquity shall be scattered.

10 But my horn shalt thou exalt like the horn of an unicorn: I shall be anointed with fresh oil.

11 Mine eye also shall see my desire on mine enemies, and mine ears shall hear my desire of the wicked that rise up against me.

12 The righteous shall flourish like the palm tree: he shall grow like a cedar in Lebanon.

13 Those that be planted in the house of the LORD shall flourish in the courts of our God.

14 They shall still bring forth fruit in old age; they shall be fat and flourishing;

15 To shew that the LORD is upright: he is my rock, and there is no unrighteousness in him.

Psalm 103

1 Bless the LORD, O my soul: and all that is within me, bless his holy name.

2 Bless the LORD, O my soul, and forget not all his benefits:

3 Who forgiveth all thine iniquities; who healeth all thy diseases;

4 Who redeemeth thy life from destruction; who crowneth thee with lovingkindness and tender mercies;

5 Who satisfieth thy mouth with good things; so that thy youth is renewed like the eagle's.

6 The LORD executeth righteousness and judgment for all that are oppressed.

7 He made known his ways unto Moses, his acts unto the children of Israel.

8 The LORD is merciful and gracious, slow to anger, and plenteous in mercy.

9 He will not always chide: neither will he keep his anger for ever.

10 He hath not dealt with us after our sins; nor rewarded us according to our iniquities.

11 For as the heaven is high above the earth, so great is his mercy toward them that fear him.

12 As far as the east is from the west, so far hath he removed our transgressions from us.

13 Like as a father pitieth his children, so the LORD pitieth them that fear him.

14 For he knoweth our frame; he remembereth that we are dust.

15 As for man, his days are as grass: as a flower of the field, so he flourisheth.

16 For the wind passeth over it, and it is gone; and the place thereof shall know it no more.

17 But the mercy of the LORD is from everlasting to everlasting upon them that fear him, and his righteousness unto children's children;

18 To such as keep his covenant, and to those that remember his commandments to do them.

19 The LORD hath prepared his throne in the heavens; and his kingdom ruleth over all.

20 Bless the LORD, ye his angels, that excel in strength, that do his commandments, hearkening unto the voice of his word.

21 Bless ye the LORD, all ye his hosts; ye ministers of his, that do his pleasure.

22 Bless the LORD, all his works in all places of his dominion: bless the LORD, O my soul.

Psalm 121

1 I will lift up mine eyes unto the hills, from whence cometh my help.

2 My help cometh from the LORD, which made heaven and earth.

3 He will not suffer thy foot to be moved: he that keepeth thee will not slumber.

4 Behold, he that keepeth Israel shall neither slumber nor sleep.

5 The LORD is thy keeper: the LORD is thy shade upon thy right hand.

6 The sun shall not smite thee by day, nor the moon by night.

7 The LORD shall preserve thee from all evil: he shall preserve thy soul.

8 The LORD shall preserve thy going out and thy coming in from this time forth, and even for evermore.

Psalm 124

1 If it had not been the LORD who was on our side, now may Israel say;

2 If it had not been the LORD who was on our side, when men rose up against us:

3 Then they had swallowed us up quick, when their wrath was kindled against us:

4 Then the waters had overwhelmed us, the stream had gone over our soul:

5 Then the proud waters had gone over our soul.

6 Blessed be the LORD, who hath not given us as a prey to their teeth.

7 Our soul is escaped as a bird out of the snare of the fowlers: the snare is broken, and we are escaped.

8 Our help is in the name of the LORD, who made heaven and earth.

Psalm 126

1 When the LORD turned again the captivity of Zion, we were like them that dream.

2 Then was our mouth filled with laughter, and our tongue with singing: then said they among the heathen, The LORD hath done great things for them.

3 The LORD hath done great things for us; whereof we are glad.

4 Turn again our captivity, O LORD, as the streams in the south.

5 They that sow in tears shall reap in joy.

6 He that goeth forth and weepeth, bearing precious seed, shall doubtless come again with rejoicing, bringing his sheaves with him.

Psalm 127

1 Except the LORD build the house, they labour in vain that build it: except the LORD keep the city, the watchman waketh but in vain.

2 It is vain for you to rise up early, to sit up late, to eat the bread of sorrows: for so he giveth his beloved sleep.

3 Lo, children are an heritage of the LORD: and the fruit of the womb is his reward.

4 As arrows are in the hand of a mighty man; so are children of the youth.

5 Happy is the man that hath his quiver full of them: they shall not be ashamed, but they shall speak with the enemies in the gate.

Psalm 128

1 Blessed is every one that feareth the LORD; that walketh in his ways.

2 For thou shalt eat the labour of thine hands: happy shalt thou be, and it shall be well with thee.

3 Thy wife shall be as a fruitful vine by the sides of thine house: thy children like olive plants round about thy table.

4 Behold, that thus shall the man be blessed that feareth the LORD.

5 The LORD shall bless thee out of Zion: and thou shalt see the good of Jerusalem all the days of thy life.

6 Yea, thou shalt see thy children's children, and peace upon Israel.

Postscript

I am adding a postscript to this book to encourage you, if you have been blessed and challenged by this book, to please write to us here at our Tampa office or email us at testimonies@revival.com We would love to hear from you. If you were stirred up and challenged to change and allow God to do His work in you, we pray that God would use you in a wonderful way to touch a lost and dying world.

Write:

Revival Ministries International
P.O. Box 292888
Tampa, FL 33687

You can also reach me at www.revival.com/prayer/testimony.aspx or call 1(813) 971-9999.

For souls and another great
spiritual awakening in America,
Dr. Rodney Howard-Browne

Information Page

For a listing of Drs. Rodney and Adonica Howard-Browne's products and itinerary, please visit revival.com

To download the soul-winning tools for free, please, visit revival.com and click on soulwinning tools or go to www.revival.com/soulwinning-tools.24.1.html

For more information about The River at Tampa Bay Church, the River Bible Institute, the River School of Worship, the River School of Government, and/or the Great Awakening Broadcast, please visit revival.com or call 1(813) 971-9999.

www.facebook.com/pages/Rodney-Adonica-Howard-Browne/31553452437

www.twitter.com/rhowardbrowne

www.youtube.com/user/rodneyhowardbrowne

About the Author

Drs. Rodney and Adonica Howard-Browne are the founders of The River at Tampa Bay Church, River Bible Institute, River School of Worship, and River School of Government in Tampa, Florida.

In December, 1987, Rodney Howard-Browne, along with his wife, Adonica, and their three children, Kirsten, Kelly and Kenneth, moved from their native land, South Africa, to the United States – called by God as missionaries from Africa to America. The Lord had spoken through Rodney in a word of prophecy and declared: "As America has sown missionaries over the last 200 years, I am going to raise up people from other nations to come to the United States of America. I am sending a mighty revival to America."

Rodney and Adonica have been called by God to reach out to the nations, but America is their primary mission field, and ministry to the people of this great land, is their priority. Their heart is to see the Church – the Body of Christ – revived, and the lost won to Christ. They have conducted several mass-crusades and many outreaches, but their heart is to train and equip others to bring in the harvest – from one-on-one evangelism to outreaches that reach tens, hundreds, thousands, and even tens of thousands. Every soul matters and every salvation is a victory for the kingdom of God!

In 1998, God gave Pastor Rodney a supernatural dream about a huge soul-winning crusade in New York City. In the summer of 1999, they rented Madison Square Garden for six weeks of focused soul-winning, under the banner of Good News New York. There was street witnessing by day and Gospel meetings at night. During this event, 48,459 people made Jesus the Lord of their lives (recorded decisions) and hundreds were trained on how to win souls for Christ. This was just the beginning of a mighty harvest that is still coming in!

Drs. Rodney and Adonica's second daughter, Kelly, was born with an incurable lung disease, called Cystic Fibrosis. This demonic disease slowly destroyed her lungs. Early on Christmas morning 2002, at the age of eighteen, she ran out of lung capacity and breathed her last breath. They placed her into the arms of her Lord and Savior and then vowed a vow. First, they vowed that the devil would pay for what he had done to their family. Secondly, they vowed to do everything in their power, with the help of the Lord, to win 100 million souls to Jesus and to put $1 billion into world missions and the harvest of souls!

With a passion for souls and a passion to revive and mobilize the body of Christ, Drs. Rodney and Adonica have conducted soul-winning efforts throughout America and other countries with "Good News" campaigns, R.M.I. Revivals, and the Great Awakening Tours (G.A.T.). As a result, millions have come to Christ and tens of thousands of believers have been revived, and also mobilized, to preach the Gospel of Jesus Christ. So far, around the world, over 8,700,000 people have made decisions for Jesus Christ!

In January 2011, the Great Awakening Broadcast was launched. This gave the ministry of Drs. Rodney and Adonica the opportunity to reach out and preach the Gospel into more than 40-million homes, by way of satellite, on Dish and Directv, CTN and CTNI, plus other stations across North, Central, and South America. This massive soul-winning effort was initiated by two ministries